GW01551134

· FUN · WITH · MAT

MEASURING

LAKSHMI HEWAVISENTI

Gloucester Press

London · New York · Toronto · Sydney

© Aladdin Books Ltd 1991

All rights reserved

Created and designed by
N.W. Books
28 Percy Street
London W1P 9FF

Design: David West
Children's Book Design
Editor: Melanie Halton
Illustrators: John Kelly
Ian Moores

*First published in Great Britain
in 1991 by*
Franklin Watts Ltd
96 Leonard Street
London
EC2A 4RH

ISBN 0-7496-0558-8

Printed in Belgium

A CIP catalogue record for this
book is available from the British
Library.

CONTENTS

NORFOLK LIBRARY AND
INFORMATION SERVICE

SUPPLIER	ASKEW
INVOICE No.	59734
ORDER DATE	8-11-91
COPY No.	

J530.8

INTRODUCTION

Is the distance around your hand longer than your arm? Which of your friends can run the fastest? You'll learn how to find these answers in this book – and try lots of other measuring activities which are enjoyable to do. Learning how to measure can be really good fun – and you can learn lots of new things at the same time!

VOLUME

If an apple were hollow, would it hold more water than a cup? There is a way to find out which one has more volume (holds more) – try this experiment with other objects too.

Measuring volume
Put the apple in the jug and cover it with water. Write down the number that the water reaches on the jug. Now remove the apple and note the new number on the jug. Do a take away sum to find the volume of the apple.

What you need

Measuring jug   Mixing bowl

Plastic bottle   Baking tray

Egg
Stone
Apple   Pencil
Tomato   Ruler
Paper

Hand volume
Use the same method to measure the volume of lots of things, including your hand. Try it for bigger hands too!

Make a graph

Guess and measure the volumes of the other objects. Then draw a chart like this one to show your results.

MILLILITRES

70
60
50
40
30
20
10
0

BALL EGG STONE APPLE TOMATO POTATO

Guessing the volume

Guess the volumes of each container. Now fill them with water. Empty each one into the jug and check the numbers to see if your guesses were right.

Pour water into each of the containers.

Bowl

Washing-up bottle with top cut off

Egg-cup

Baking tray

SIZE & WEIGHT

If two objects have the same weight, do you think they have to have the same size? Here is an experiment you could do to see if you are right.

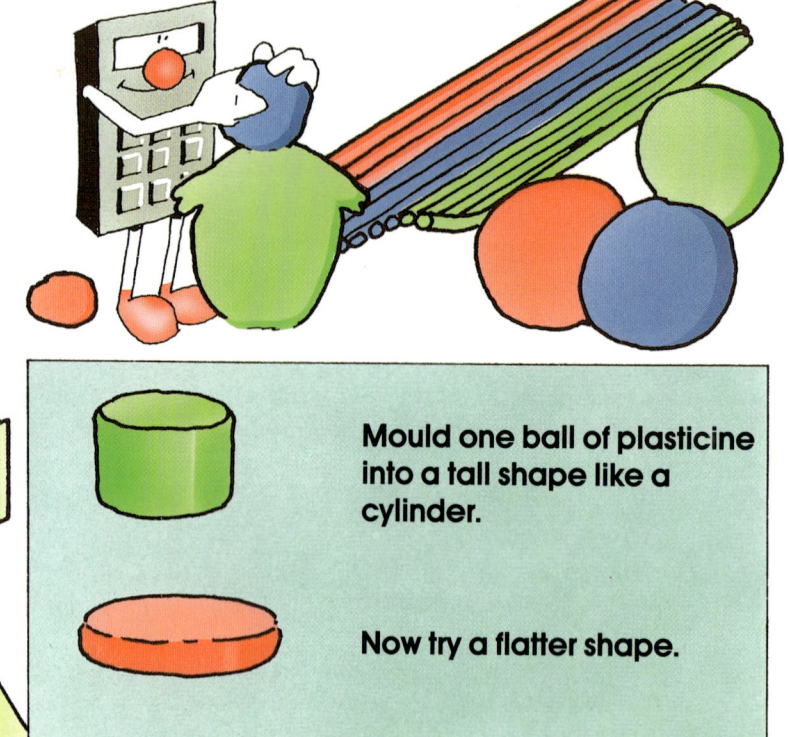

What you need
Ruler
Scales
Measuring jug
Plasticine

What to do
To begin with, weigh out three equal balls of plasticine. Make sure they weigh exactly the same. Now mould them into three different shapes.

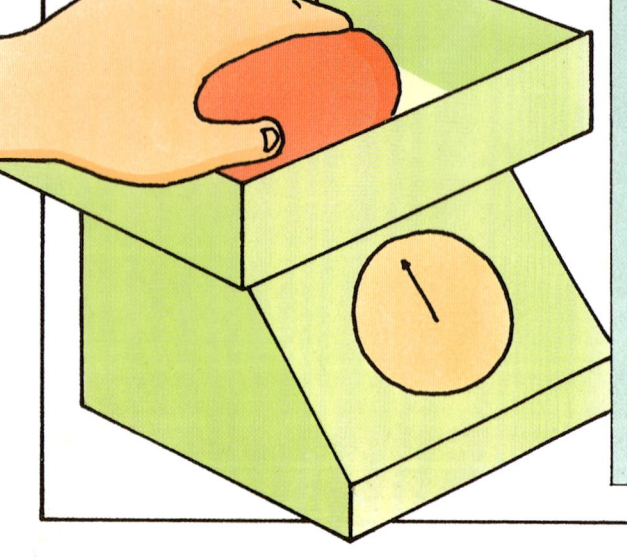

Mould one ball of plasticine into a tall shape like a cylinder.

Now try a flatter shape.

You could also try a very flat shape (like a pancake).

Estimating volume

Try putting your three shapes into a jug of water. Make sure the water covers your shape without spilling out of the jug. Does the water level go up to the same mark for all three shapes?

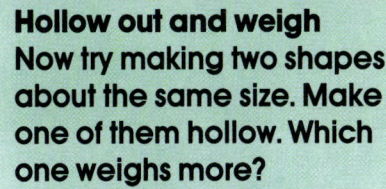

Hollow out and weigh

Now try making two shapes about the same size. Make one of them hollow. Which one weighs more?

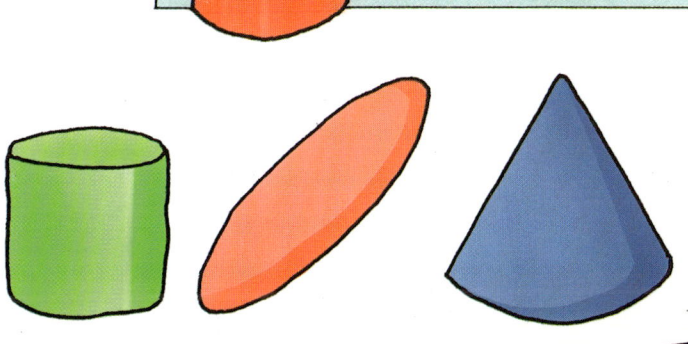

The same volume?

Using your three equal pieces of plasticine, make the thick, medium and thin shapes shown here. Check their volumes – did you think they would be the same?

TEMPERATURE

These are activities which will give you an idea of how long water takes to get cold...or turn to ice.

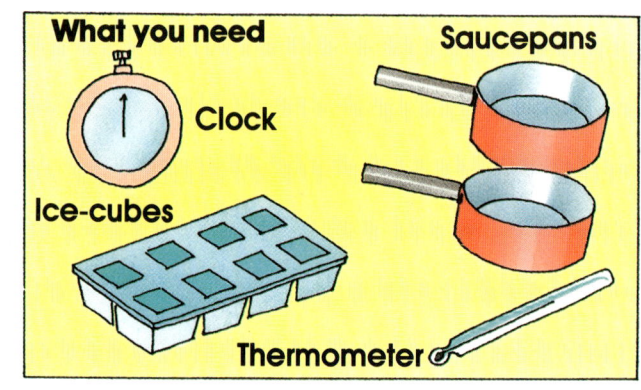

What you need

Clock

Saucepans

Ice-cubes

Thermometer

Fill two saucepans with equal amounts of water.

Put ice into one.

Take the temperature in both pans every five minutes.

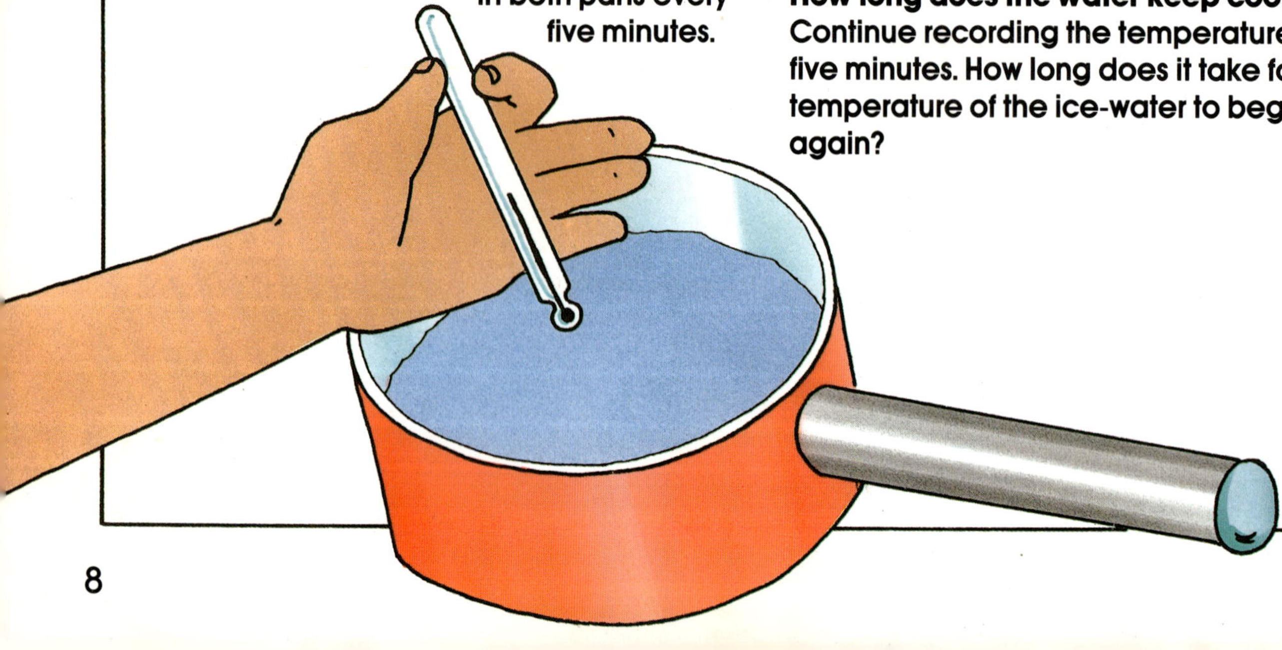

How long does the water keep cooling?
Continue recording the temperatures every five minutes. How long does it take for the temperature of the ice-water to begin to rise again?

How fast will water freeze?

For this experiment, you will need two plastic beakers. Put some water into each one, and add some salt to one of them. Make sure that both the beakers have about the same amount of water in them.

What you need

Water

Plastic beakers

Salt

Put both containers in the freezer. Guess which one will freeze first, and keep checking every half hour or so. Then, when you see signs of the water freezing, check them every five minutes.

Did they both freeze?
Which one froze more quickly?
What does salt do?

Were you right?
How long did it take?

9

SPEED

Speed is another way of saying "how fast". So your running speed is higher than your walking speed. This activity shows you how you can measure your speed.

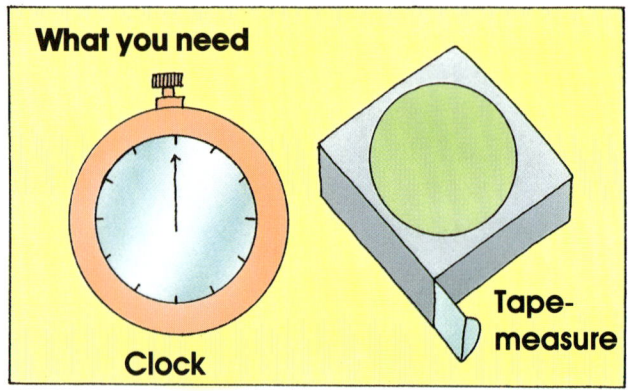

What you need

Clock

Tape-measure

What to do
Mark a starting line. Ask a friend to start the clock and shout "Go". When you hear this, run as fast as you can.

After ten seconds, your friend should shout "Stop". Mark the point you have reached. Now measure the distance you ran.

10 SECONDS

20 METRES

If you could keep running at this speed, you could run double this distance in 20 seconds. So if you run 20 metres in 10 seconds, your distance in 20 seconds would be twice as far – 40 metres.

Try this
If you pretend that you can keep running at the same speed indefinitely, you can work out how far you could run in any time period.

30 SECS.

3 × 20 = 60 METRES

How many metres per minute?
There are 60 seconds in a minute, so to find your distance per minute, multiply six times the distance you ran in ten seconds.

1 MINUTE

6 × 20 = 120 METRES

How many metres per hour?
There are 60 minutes in an hour. Multiply your last answer by 60 to find out how far you can run in an hour (... × 60 = ... metres per hour). You can time your friends in the same way (and work out their speeds), or see what your speeds are when you hop or skip for ten seconds.

120 METRES
× 60
7200 METRES PER HOUR

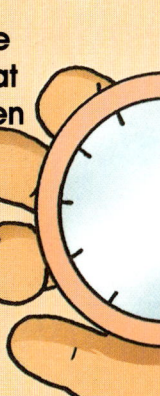

TIME AND DISTANCE

This activity is a bit like the one you did for speed (pg.10-11), but slightly different – this time you stop when you are ready, and not when your friend tells you to!

What you need

Calculator

Watch

Paper

Tape-measure

Pencil

Use a tape-measure to mark out a distance of 30 metres. Get your friend to time how long you take to walk to the other end.

30 metres

Let's say you took ten seconds. How far had you walked in half the time (five seconds)? In one second? How long would it take you to walk 60 metres? 120 metres?

10 SECS. = 30 M
5 SECS. = 15 m
1 SEC. = 3 m

Time your bath time

Bath times can give you a lot of information too! Time how long it takes to fill up the tub. After your bath, decide if the tub will empty in the same time as it took to fill. Check by letting the water out!

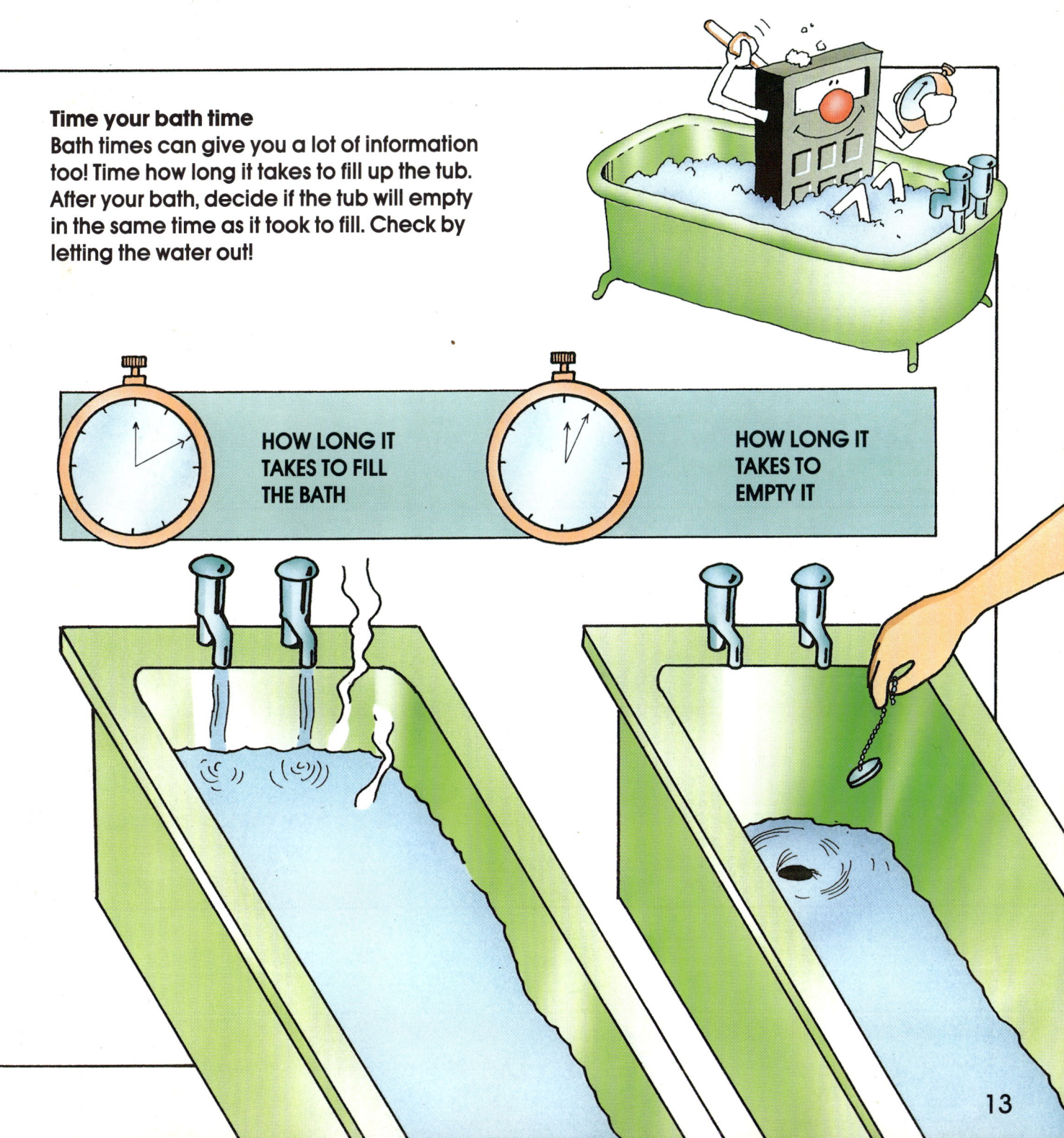

HOW LONG IT TAKES TO FILL THE BATH

HOW LONG IT TAKES TO EMPTY IT

JUDGING DISTANCE

What can you use to help you guess distances? It depends on whether you want to measure a short, medium or long distance. Try these ideas.

Medium distance

Find a pavement with several parked cars. Use the cars to help you to judge distance. Measure the first car and use this as a guide for the lengths of the others.

$$\begin{array}{r} 90\,cm \\ \times 3 \\ \hline 270\,cm \end{array}$$

$$\begin{array}{r} 4\,m \\ \times 3 \\ \hline 12\,m \end{array}$$

Short distance

Find a path with paving stones. Throw a stone gently from a start line. How many squares away has it landed? Measure one square – can you now guess how far away your stone is?

Long distance
You could use a similar method to this in order to judge longer distances – lamp-posts, houses or pylons would help you here.

Far away
You can even have a rough guess at the distance to the top of a tall building. Measure the distance from the ground to the top of the first row of windows. Now count how many rows you see and multiply that figure times your measurement.

LENGTH & DISTANCE

Sometimes rulers are not the best tools to use for measuring. Tape-measures are useful for long distances, and string is good for things which are not straight.

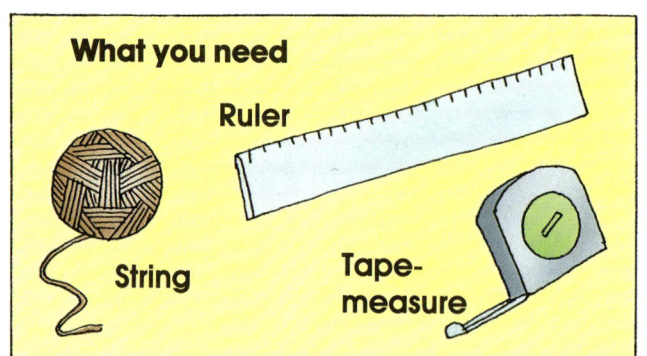

What you need

Ruler

String

Tape-measure

Measure distance
Make a mark from here, and gently throw a ball. Guess how far away it lands. Now use a tape-measure to find the distance. Was your guess right?

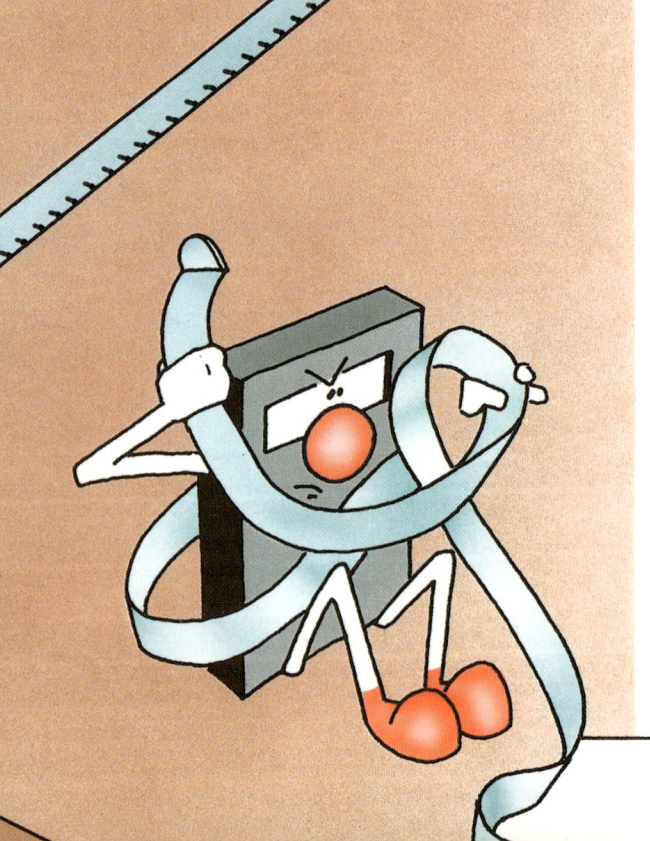

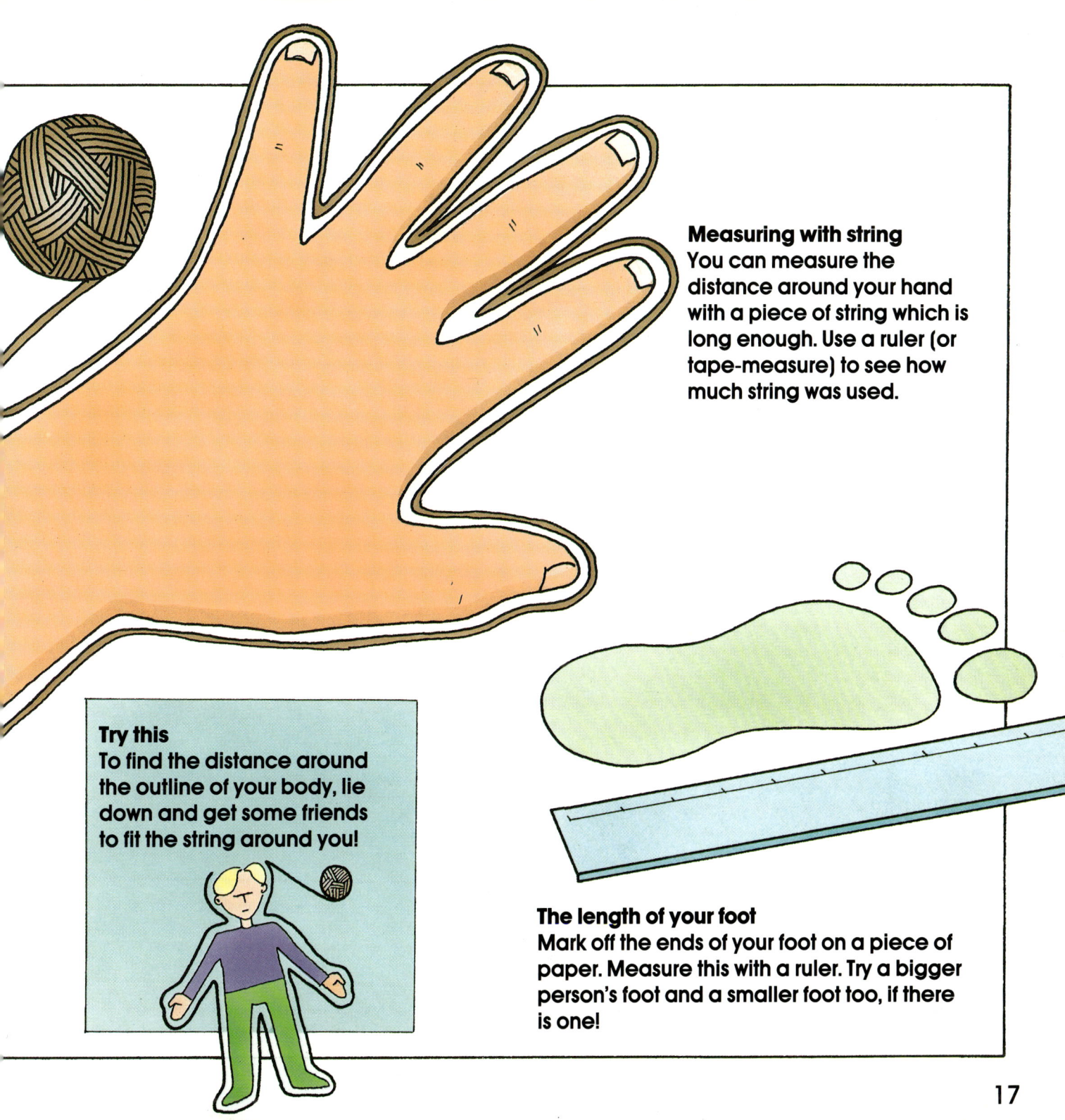

Measuring with string
You can measure the distance around your hand with a piece of string which is long enough. Use a ruler (or tape-measure) to see how much string was used.

Try this
To find the distance around the outline of your body, lie down and get some friends to fit the string around you!

The length of your foot
Mark off the ends of your foot on a piece of paper. Measure this with a ruler. Try a bigger person's foot and a smaller foot too, if there is one!

WAYS OF MEASURING

Before people invented rulers, they used other objects for measuring. Parts of the body were often used, and even today people use "paces" or "hands" to measure some things.

What you need

String

Pencils

Spaghetti

What to do
See how much string you need to go around your head. Measure the string with a ruler. Try measuring other round things. Use spaghetti for straight things, like your table or bed. Measure your room in "paces".

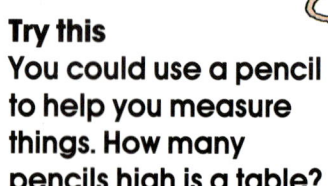

Try this
You could use a pencil to help you measure things. How many pencils high is a table?

Use other things to measure
You can measure with a pencil, some string or spaghetti. Then measure them with a ruler.

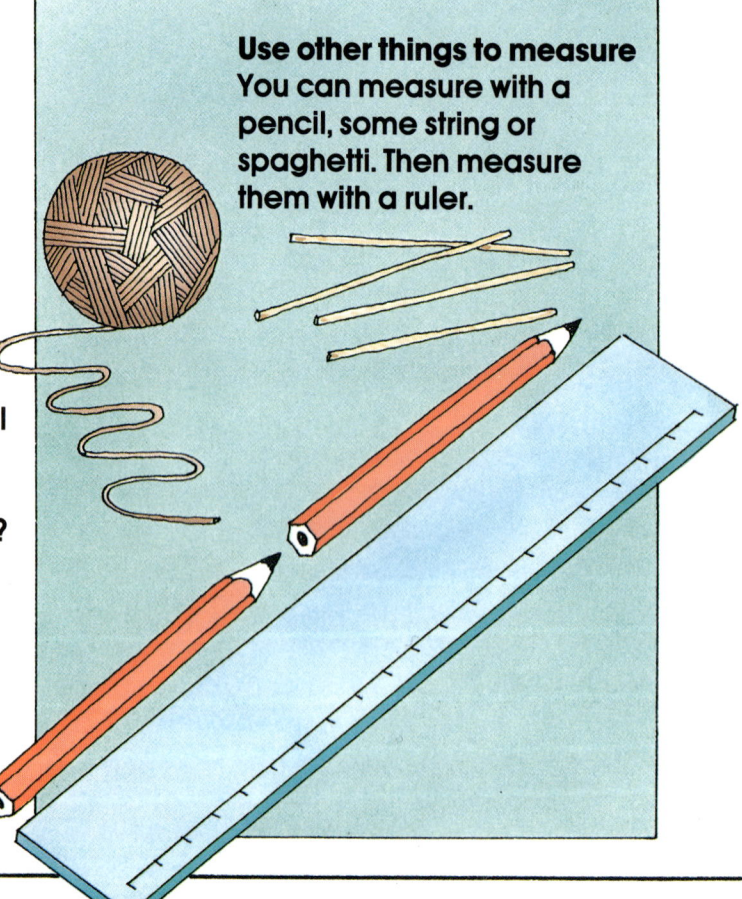

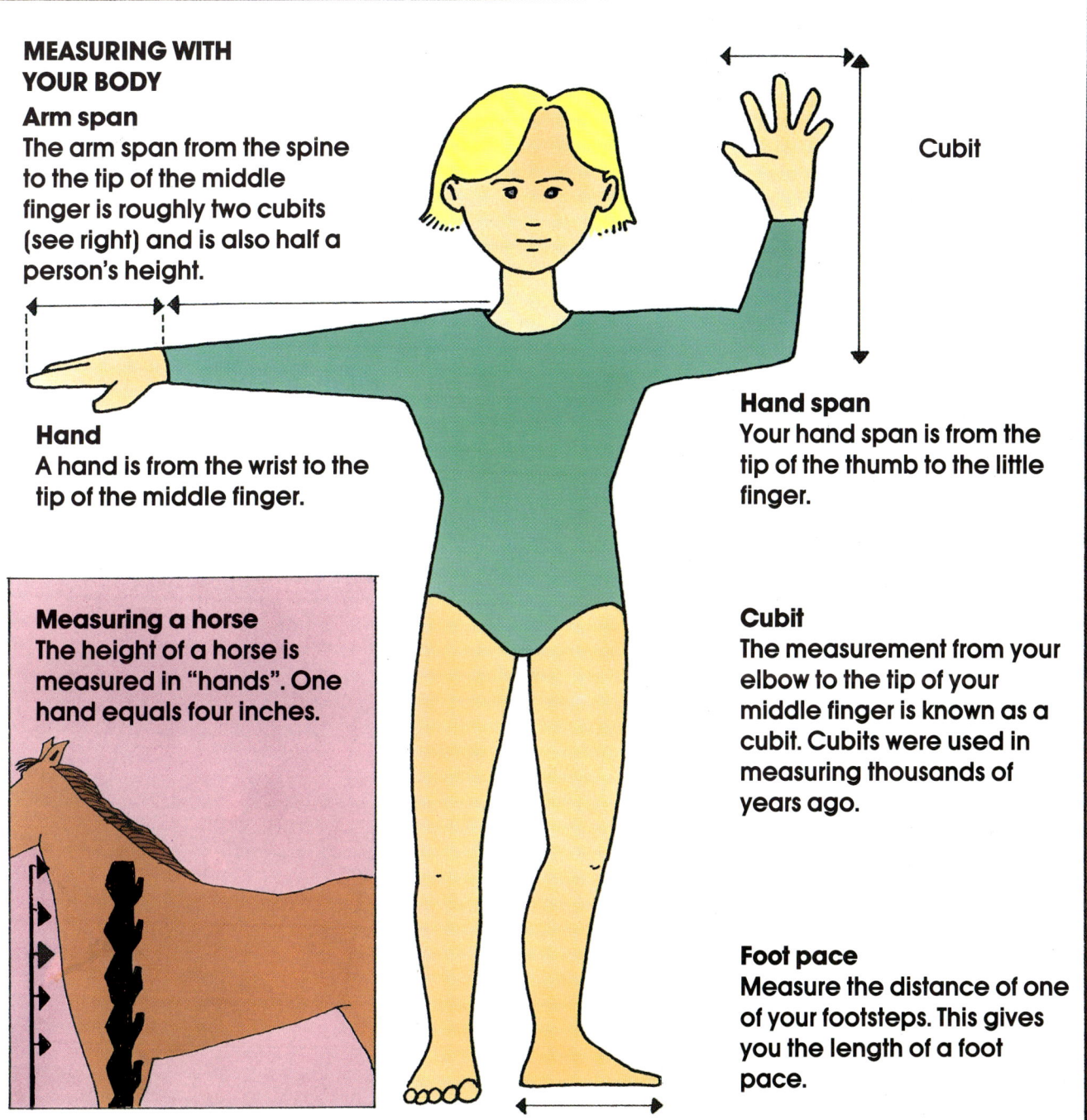

MEASURING WITH YOUR BODY

Arm span
The arm span from the spine to the tip of the middle finger is roughly two cubits (see right) and is also half a person's height.

Hand
A hand is from the wrist to the tip of the middle finger.

Cubit

Hand span
Your hand span is from the tip of the thumb to the little finger.

Cubit
The measurement from your elbow to the tip of your middle finger is known as a cubit. Cubits were used in measuring thousands of years ago.

Measuring a horse
The height of a horse is measured in "hands". One hand equals four inches.

Foot pace
Measure the distance of one of your footsteps. This gives you the length of a foot pace.

AREA

To compare and measure the area (the size of the surface) of different shapes, draw them on to graph paper and then count the squares.

What you need

Graph paper

Newspaper

Pencil   Ruler

Draw round your hand on to squared paper

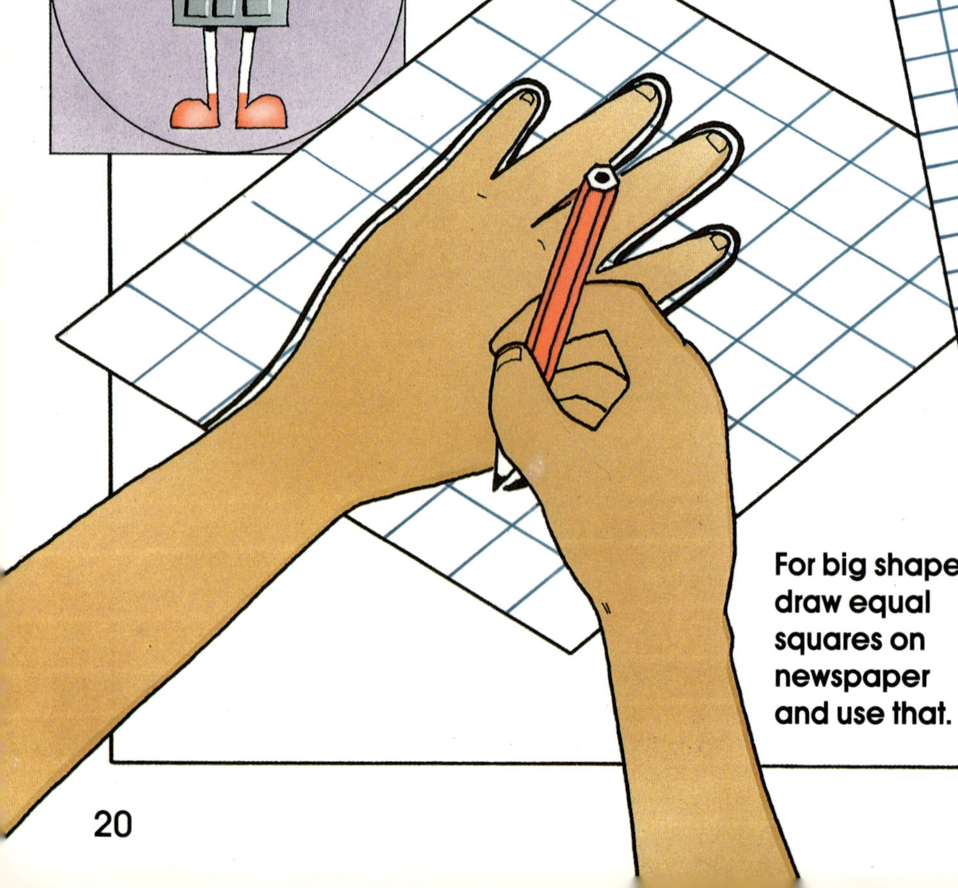

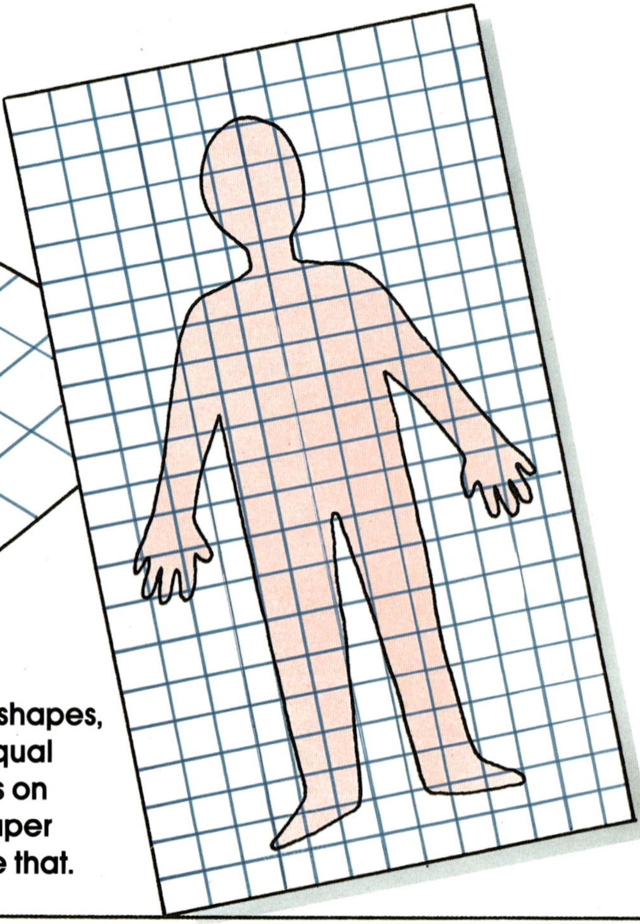

For big shapes, draw equal squares on newspaper and use that.

20

Measure your bedroom
You can make an accurate drawing of your bedroom using graph paper. First, measure your room and the furniture. Now draw it all in position. Each 1cm square of the paper could represent, say, 15cm.

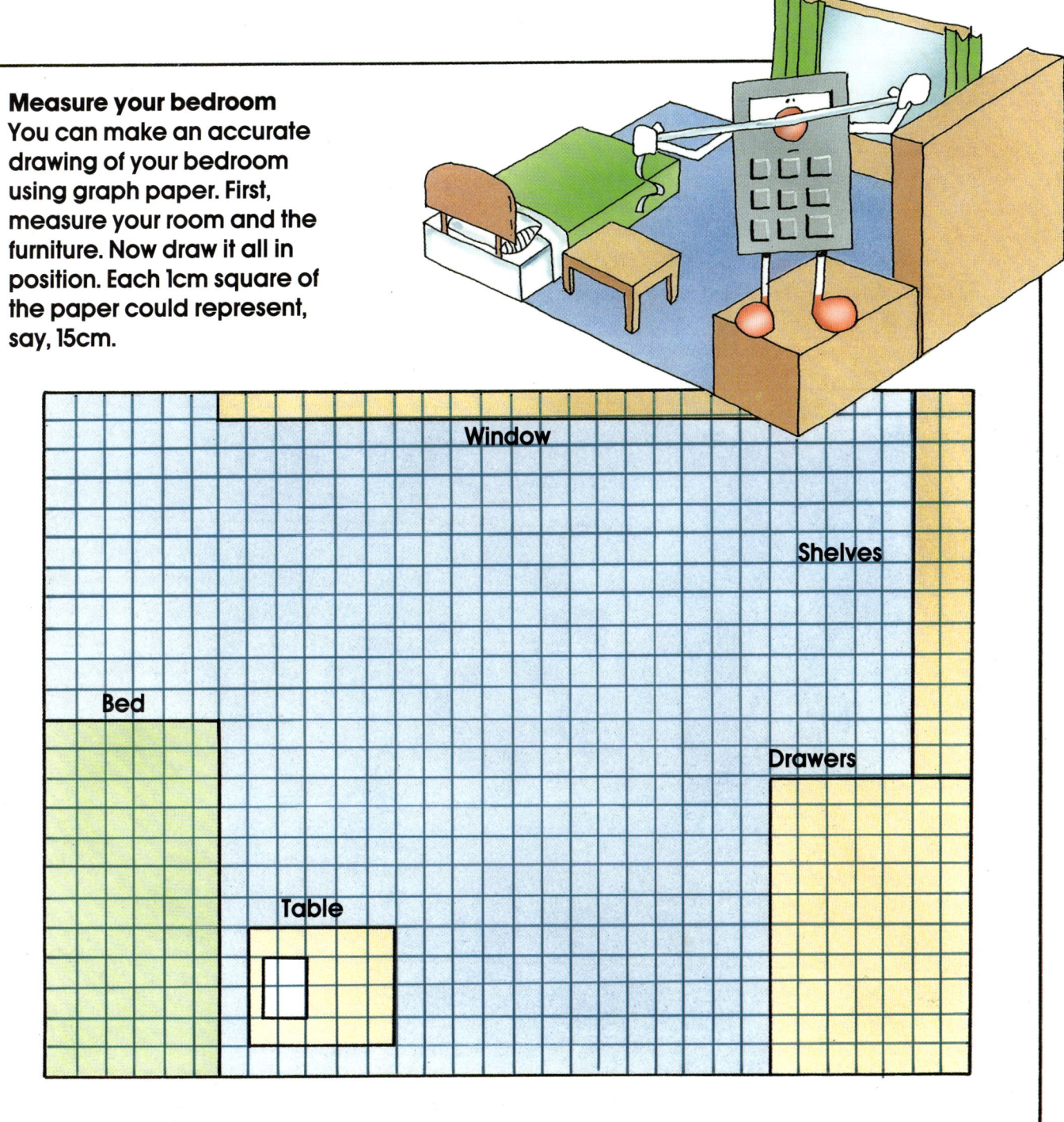

Window

Shelves

Bed

Drawers

Table

WEIGHING

Can you always tell which is the heavier of two things just by holding or looking at them? In this activity you check weights to see how close your guesses were.

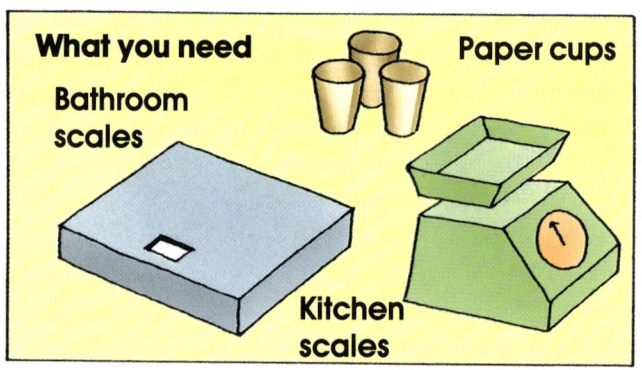

What you need

Bathroom scales

Paper cups

Kitchen scales

Estimating weight
First find several objects like these and put them in a line from lightest to heaviest (guess the order by feeling and comparing the objects). Now check by using scales.

Size and weight

Does a cup of rice weigh the same as a cup of flour? Try filling some paper cups with different things like salt, peas, peanuts, and so on. Guess the order from the lightest to the heaviest. Check each one with the scales. Were you right?

Salt

Peas

Popcorn

Rice

Peanuts

Sand

Flour

Weighing yourself

Try recording your weight each month for a year. Draw a chart like this and mark it on the first day of each month.

Weight in kgs.

27
26
25
24
23
22
21
20

1 2 3 4 5 6 7 8 9 10 11 12
MONTHS

23

STRAW SCALES

Have you ever thought about making your own scales to compare the weights of small things like paperclips, peas and matchsticks? Here is how you can make some straw scales.

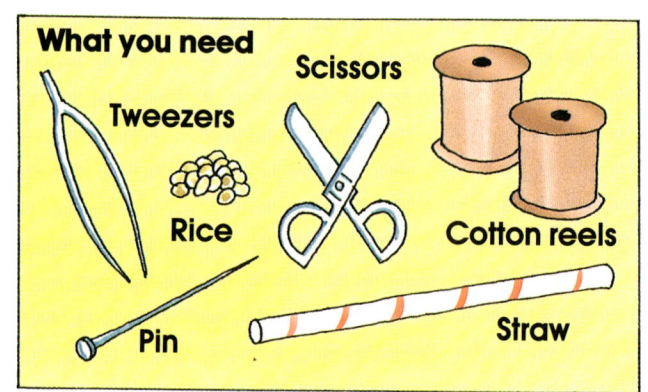

What you need

Tweezers

Rice

Scissors

Cotton reels

Pin

Straw

First step
Cut out a scoop at both ends of the straw. Make sure they match in size.

How to make your scales
Push a pin through the middle of the straw and balance it on two cotton reels, as below. If it doesn't balance, put a small paper 'rider', or loop, on the higher side and move it around until you get perfect balance.

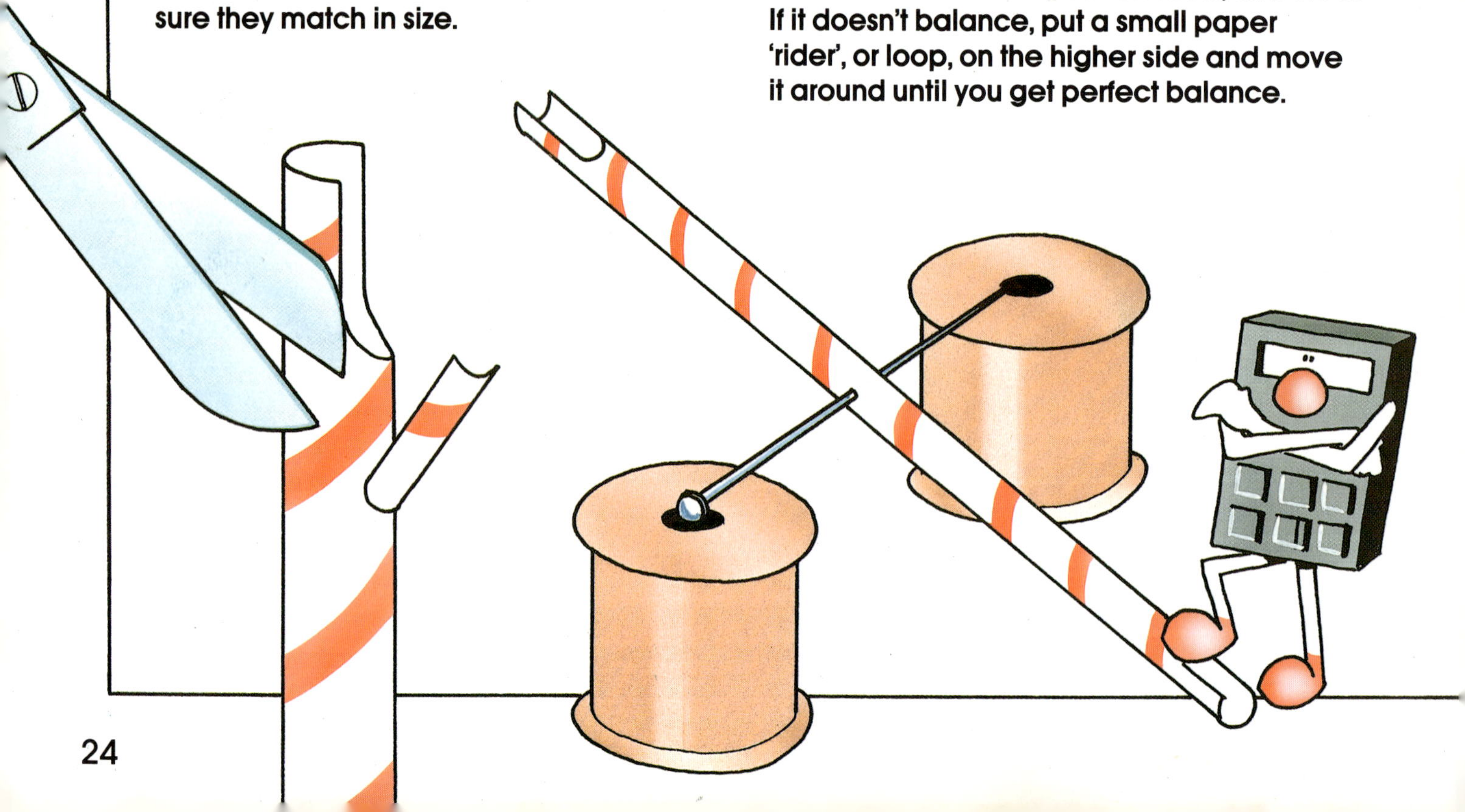

Things to measure

Now try weighing something small, like a peanut, by putting it into one of the scoops. Balance your scales with grains of rice on the other side. You will need to be gentle and use tweezers. Make a note of how many rice grains you use. Weigh other objects in the same way.

Try this

You could compare the weights of bigger objects by using a large card tube instead of a straw.

5 GRAINS OF RICE = 1 PEANUT

WEIGHING-RULER

This is an experiment which will help you compare the weights of different objects without using any weighing scales. Instead you will use a weighing-ruler.

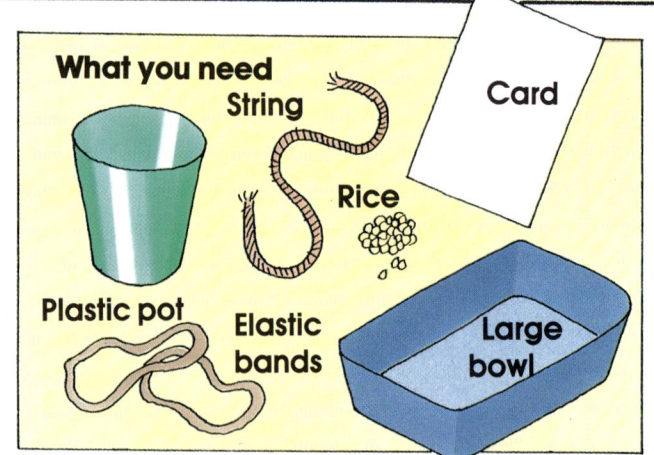

What you need
String
Card
Rice
Plastic pot
Elastic bands
Large bowl

How to make it
Put the string through the elastic band and tie it on to the pot. Now hang this on a door handle and put the bowl under it.

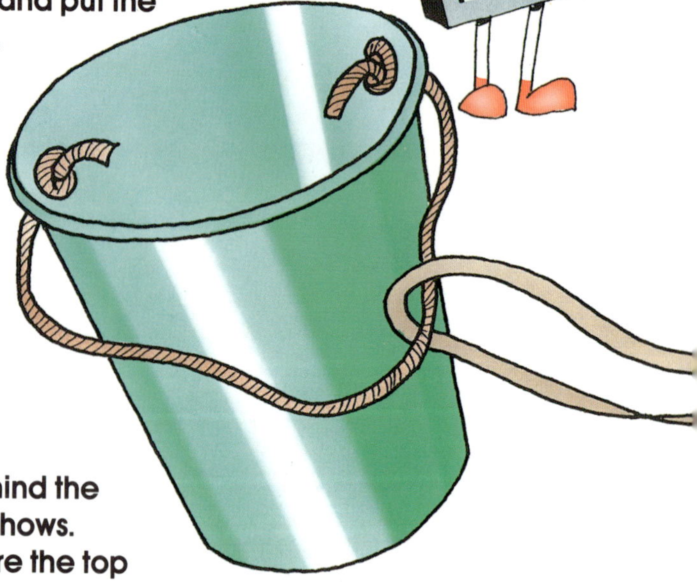

Place the card behind the pot as the picture shows. Mark the card where the top of the empty pot reaches.

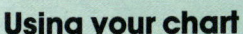

0 ——
spoonfuls

5 ——
spoonfuls

10 ——
spoonfuls

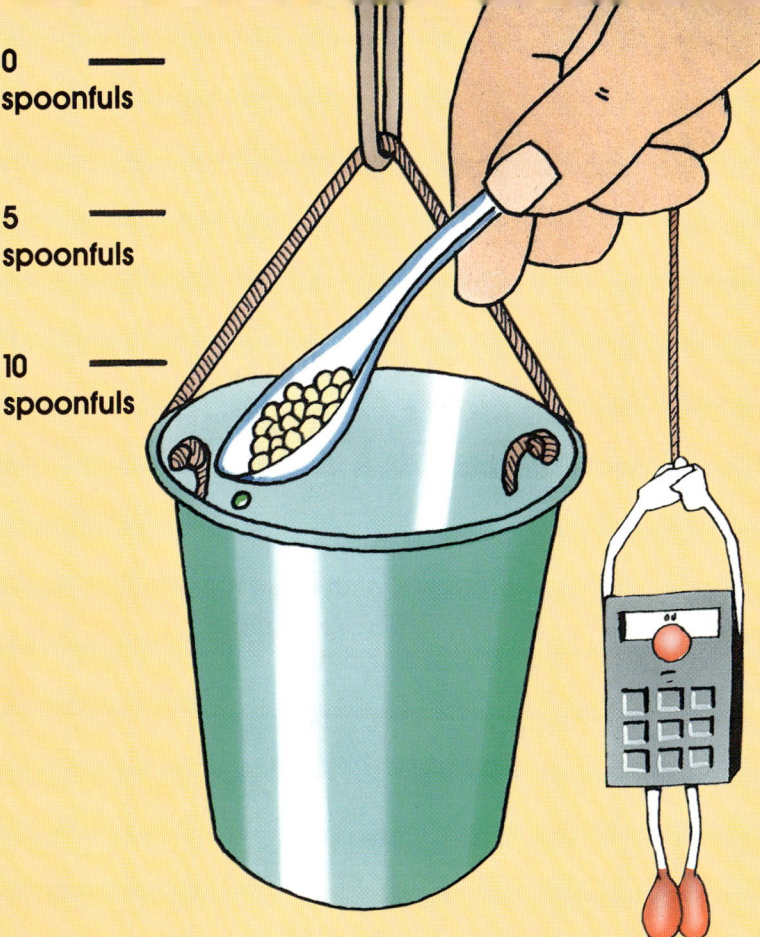

Using your chart
Use this weighing-ruler to weigh other objects. If your elastic has stretched, you will need to start again with a new one, the same size as the original elastic.

Measuring rice in cups
Now you are ready to start the experiment. Gently add five spoonfuls of rice into the pot. Mark where the top of the pot reaches now. Keep adding the rice, five spoonfuls at a time, and keep marking the card as you go along. You can also try weighing other objects, like marbles or small sweets. Keep a record of their weights on the same card and compare them.

SPEEDY SEEDS

How fast does a plant grow? Try growing plants from seeds and take measurements each day. To make it interesting, try growing one in the dark and one in the light.

What you need

Pencil

Ruler

Tray

Seeds

Cotton-wool

Growing mustard seeds
First, put cotton-wool in a plastic tray or box. Dampen the cotton-wool with water. Sprinkle the mustard seeds on top.

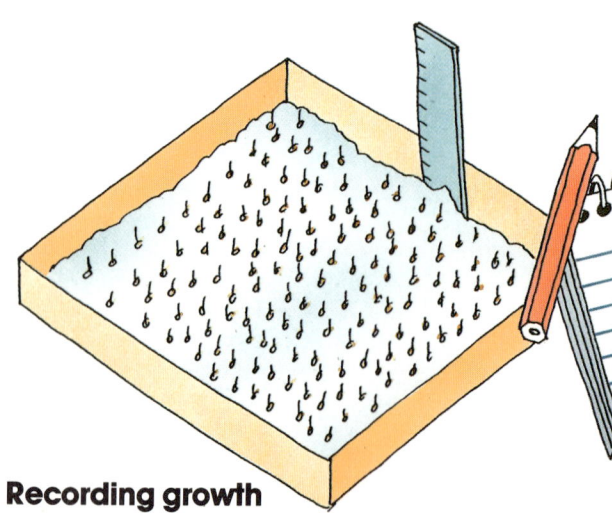

Recording growth
After two or three days you will see the shoots. Measure them each day. When did they grow most quickly? When did they stop growing?

Comparing growth

Follow the same steps again, but this time divide your tray in half. Sprinkle one half with mustard seeds and the other with cress seeds. Keep a chart of their daily heights. Which grew faster?

Try this

Use two trays and sprinkle each with one kind of seed. Cover one and put the other in a light place. Which one do you think will grow faster?

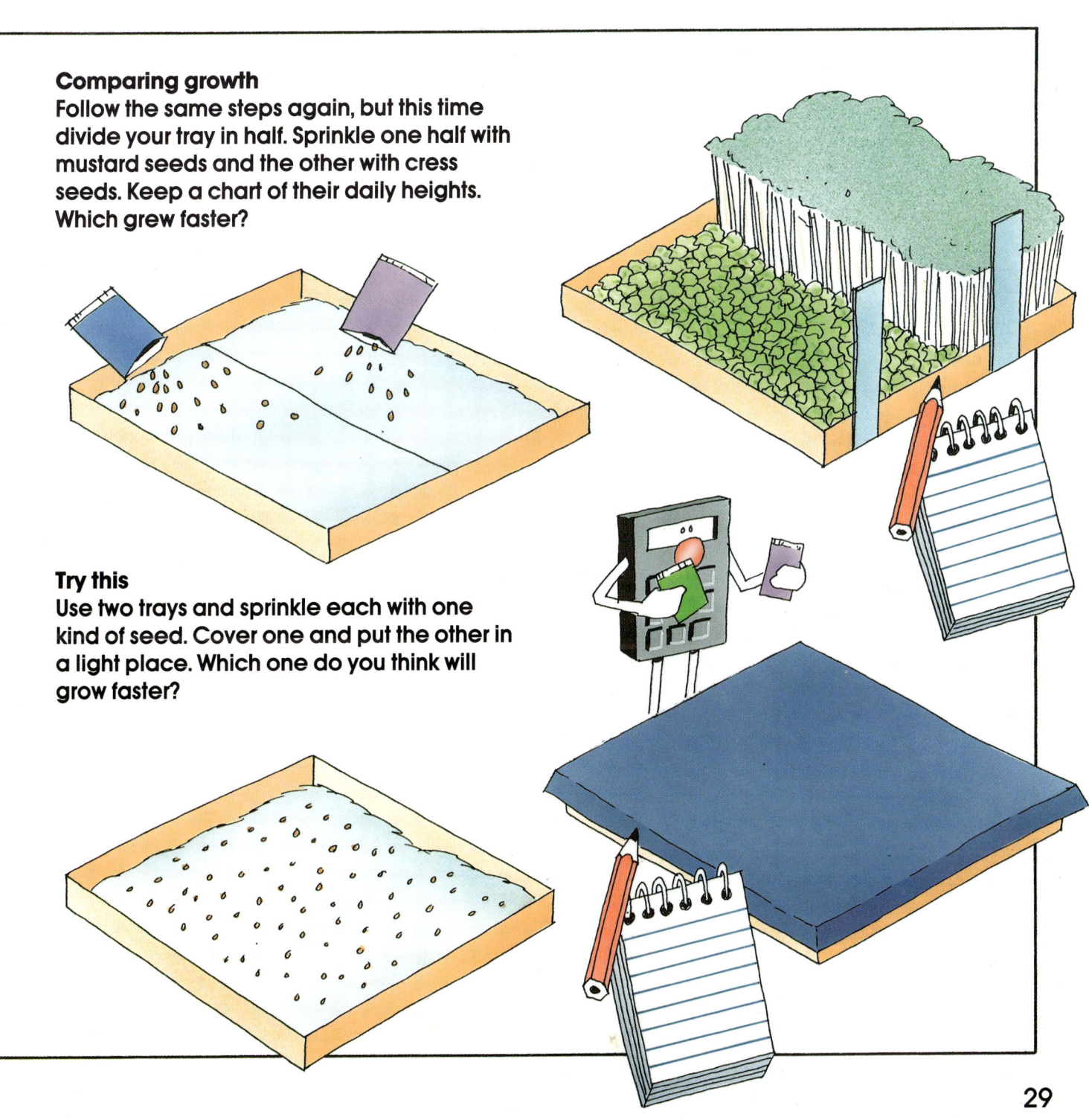

29

WEIGHTS & MEASURES

Here is a list of measuring terms and mathematical symbols which you will find helpful. As you do more maths, this information will come in handy!

ABBREVIATIONS

g = gram   oz = ounce
kg = kilogram   lb = pound

mm = millimetre   in = inch
cm = centimetre   ft = foot
m = metre   yd = yard
km = kilometre   mi = mile

ml = millilitre   fl oz = fluid ounce
l = litre   pt = pint

WEIGHT

1,000g = 1kg   16oz = 1lb
       1kg   2lb 3oz

LENGTH/DISTANCE

10mm = 1cm   12in = 1ft
100cm = 1m   36in = 1yd
1,000mm = 1m   3ft = 1yd
1,000m = 1km   5,280ft = 1mi
       1km   ⅗mi = 3,279ft

VOLUME

1,000ml = 1l   20fl oz = 1 pt

TIME

60 seconds	=	1 minute
15 minutes	=	¼ hour
30 minutes	=	½ hour
60 minutes	=	1 hour
24 hours	=	1 day
365 days	=	1 year

ABBREVIATIONS

sec	=	second
min	=	minute
hr	=	hour
yr	=	year

ARITHMETIC SIGNS

+   ADDITION (plus)

—   SUBTRACTION (minus)

×   MULTIPLICATION (multiply by)

÷   DIVISION (divide by)

=   EQUALITY (equals)

INDEX

ANSWERS

Page 9: Salt water freezes more slowly.

Page 12: If you took 10 seconds to walk 30m, in 5 secs. you walked 15m; in one sec. you walked 3m. To walk 60m, you would take 20 secs.; 120m would take 40 secs.

PRINTED IN BELGIUM BY
proost
INTERNATIONAL BOOK PRODUCTION